100 Questions and Answers About African Americans

Michigan State University School of Journalism

Read The Spirit Books

an imprint of
David Crumm Media, LLC
Canton, Michigan

For more information and further discussion, visit
http://news.jrn.msu.edu/culturalcompetence/

Cover art and design by
Rick Nease
www.RickNeaseArt.com

Published By
Read The Spirit Books
an imprint of
David Crumm Media, LLC
42015 Ford Rd., Suite 234
Canton, Michigan, USA

For information about customized editions, bulk purchases
or permissions, contact David Crumm Media, LLC at info@
DavidCrummMedia.com

Contents

Preface

This guide was created amid demonstrations on U.S. streets and campuses. People were protesting the killings and violent arrests of African Americans by some police. Social media campaigns including #BlackLivesMatter and #ICantBreathe fueled the protests. During the week after this class began, students at the University of Missouri-Columbia marched against racism. The college movement leaped through #BlackOnCampus and other channels. Soon, students called for greater racial equity at more than 70 universities, including our own campus.

We intended for this guide to encourage understanding and conversation. This is what journalism should do. The protests made us more keenly aware of how important this project is and how simple answers are ill suited for complicated issues. We added, dropped, reworded and reordered questions. We researched the meanings of single words, discussed questions and answers and considered the accuracy of the overall impression this guide would convey.

As this guide took shape, a Black president recognized the 150th anniversary of the Constitutional amendment abolishing formal slavery. Despite the resilience of African Americans to climb from bondage to the White House, inequity persists. As we worked, news reports showed deepening wealth disparity and growing pessimism about race relations. Many African Americans are being left behind. There are no one-size-fits-all answers and no singularly authentic Black experience. There has been progress, but we have far to go.

This turmoil about longstanding racial inequities has been the context for our work. We hope this guide helps the national conversation. We hope it encourages people to get to know each other better and to listen.

Acknowledgments

These are the authors. Seated from left: Rachel Linnemann, Kelsey Block, Veronica Muñoz and Stephanie Hernandez McGavin. Kneeling: Paige Boyd, Caitlin Taylor, Lilliana Forti, Stacy Cornwell and Danielle Schwartz. Standing: Cayden Royce, Victoria Bowles, Rashad Timmons, Brian Batayeh, Kiana Elkins, Michelle Armstead and Brittany S. Holmes. Madeline Carino created the graphics and videos. Cody Harrell assisted with the coding.

We are especially grateful to experts who helped by answering questions or by editing our work. They helped ensure the guide's accuracy and authority. Our allies include:

Nikki G. Bannister, founder and principal editorial consultant of Nik Scott, a Gulf Coast editorial relations firm. Her career includes newspapers in Kentucky and Ohio. She has contributed to more than 10 print and online media outlets. They include The Advocate (Baton Rouge, Louisiana) and the Times-Picayune in New Orleans. She served six years and nine months as a gas turbine systems mechanic in the U.S. Navy.

Dr. Charles Corley, an associate professor in the Michigan State University Department of Criminal Justice. His doctorate is in sociology. He writes extensively on recidivism, profiling, juvenile justice, race and gender.

Dr. Pero Gaglo Dagbovie, professor of African American history and Associate Dean in the Michigan State University Graduate School. His research and teaching interests comprise a range of time periods, themes and topical specialties, including Black intellectual history, the history of the Black historical enterprise, Black women's history, the civil rights-Black Power Movement, African-American Studies, hip-hop culture, and contemporary Black history.

Joyce-Zoe Farley, a doctoral candidate in African American and African Studies with graduate certifications in journalism and digital humanities at Michigan State University. She has a bachelor's degree in broadcast journalism from Hampton University and a master's degree in oral history from Columbia University. She has experience in television, radio, newswire and newspaper writing.

Wanda J. Herndon, former senior vice president of Global Communications for Starbucks Coffee Company and founder of W Communications, a strategic communications consulting firm. For most of her 30-plus-year career, she led communications, public relations and marketing functions for leading brands and Fortune 500 companies. She has held senior-level positions at Starbucks, DuPont, The Dow Chemical Company and the Michigan House of Representatives. Herndon earned bachelor's and master's degrees from Michigan State University.

Stratton Lee, adviser in the College of Communication Arts and Sciences Department of Academic and Student Affairs at Michigan State University. He has bachelor's and master's degrees from Michigan State University and a master's in divinity studies from the Moody Bible Institute. He works on development and implementation of support networks for underserved and underrepresented people.

Walter T. Middlebrook, assistant manager editor/Metro, The Detroit News. He has been a reporter or editor for Newsday, The New York Times, USA Today, the St. Paul Pioneer Press and St. Paul Dispatch, and the Minneapolis Star. He studied at MIT, Boston University and Indiana University.

Rashad Muhammad, an instructional technologist at MSUglobal Knowledge & Learning Innovations. His bachelor's degree in telecommunication and master's degree in educational technology are from Michigan State University.

Keith Owens, senior editor of The Michigan Chronicle, an African-American newspaper founded in Detroit in 1936. He has been a reporter, editorial writer and syndicated columnist. He has worked for mainstream newspapers, an alternative weekly and a digital news site. Owens has a bachelor's degree in English from Colorado College.

Freda Sampson, director of inclusion and diversity at Blue Cross Blue Shield of Michigan. She is a community organizer and managed the Michigan Roundtable for Diversity and Inclusion's Race2Equity Program. She is also a serial entrepreneur creating intellectually social environments combining food, beverages, meeting spaces, culture and business. Sampson has a bachelor's degree in mass communication and media studies from Tennessee State University. She has also earned a master of fine arts from the University of Michigan and a leadership certificate from Harvard University's School of Divinity.

Dr. Geneva Smitherman, a university distinguished professor emerita in the departments of English and African American and African Studies at Michigan State University. She has written several books on African American Language. They include *Articulate While Black: Barack Obama, Language, and Race in the U.S.* (with H. Samy Alim, 2012), *Word From the Mother: Language and African Americans* (2006), and

Talkin' That Talk: Language, Culture and Education in African America (2000). As a guest editor, Smitherman is largely responsible for the guide's section on language.

Reginald A. Stuart, past president of the Society of Professional Journalists. He worked two decades as a corporate recruiter for Knight Ridder Newspapers and The McClatchy Co. He previously worked for Knight Ridder, The New York Times, The Philadelphia Daily News, The Tennessean and WSIX in Nashville, Tennessee. He is a winner of the Ida B. Wells Award presented by the National Association of Black Journalists and the Medill School of Journalism.

Julie Green Topping is a journalist with more than 35 years of experience, mostly in newsroom leadership. She spent most of her career at the Detroit Free Press and has worked at the Charlotte Observer, the Greensboro (North Carolina) Daily News and Record, and the Sandusky (Ohio) Register. Her website, the80percentsolution.com, encourages healthy lifestyles and diets for Black women.

Additionally, John Golaszewski of the Michigan Department of Civil Rights came to the classroom to help us frame issues and was one of our readers. We are grateful to Keith Hampton, artistic director/founder, and the Chicago Community Chorus for permission to include their recording of *Lift Ev'ry Voice and Sing*. This series has been encouraged by Paulette Granberry Russell, J.D., senior adviser to the MSU president for diversity and director of the Office for Inclusion and Intercultural Initiatives. Dr. Lucinda Davenport, professor and director of the School of Journalism, has supported this series from the beginning.

About the Series

The Michigan State University School of Journalism publishes this series of guides as a tool to replace bias and stereotypes with reliable information.

We began this guide by asking African Americans to tell us the questions and assumptions other people have about them. Some questions are simple. The answers seldom are.

At times, we must interpret questions to uncover the meaning behind them. We search for answers in studies, surveys, research and resources. We ask experts. Our goal is to answer first-level questions in ways that are accurate and clear. We hope you find questions you have had and some ideas you haven't thought about before.

By its nature, a guide like this is linear, starting at the front and running to the back. But racial issues are not linear. Often, one condition we mention early has origins or causes that are explored later. This is not a chronology. Another thing to keep in mind is that some surveys and research compare only Black people and White people. Our preference was for data comparing African Americans to the population overall, including all races and ethnicities, but that is not always available. Keep in mind that the United States is not just a binary of Black and White, but increasingly multiracial and multiethnic.

In *100 Questions and Answers About African Americans*, we capitalize Black when it refers to people with roots in Africa. For consistency, we also capitalize White as a demographic term.

Capitalization has been controversial. Some people who prefer to identify as Black want the term capitalized. They take capitalization as a sign of equality to African American, Native American, Asian American, Hispanic and Latino. Those terms are capitalized because, except for "native," all are proper nouns.

The case for lowercasing is that this is convention. This is the way it is in the Associated Press Stylebook used by many journalists. Following AP style and our mainstream peers would seem to enhance professionalism and credibility. Certainly, it wouldn't raise any questions. But no publication is bound by AP style. Many adopt exceptions that make sense for them.

For us, in the context of this series, the reasons for capitalizing Black as a racial, ethnic and cultural identifier outweigh conventions. We will capitalize Black in this and future guides in the series and as we update earlier guides.

Joe Grimm, series editor, is visiting editor in residence at Michigan State University's School of Journalism.

Identity

1 Who is this book about?

While this book is titled *100 Questions and Answers About African Americans*, it is about all people in the United States who share a lineage that can be traced directly or indirectly to Africa. Some do not identify as African American. This lineage, while collective, contains a diverse array of histories, cultures and experiences. This includes, but is not limited to, Black, African-American, Afro-Caribbean, Afro-Latino and African immigrants living in the United States. This group is not monolithic.

2 Which is preferred, Black or African American?

Either can be correct. Gallup has found since 1991 that half to two-thirds of African-American and Black respondents have not had a preference. The terms do not necessarily mean the same thing. So, it can come down to individual preferences. It is best to ask. Black and then African American replaced older terms such as Colored and Negro imposed by others. Self-identification might reflect feelings about origin, affiliation, colonialism, enslavement and cultural dispossession.

3 Why do some people prefer to identify as Black?

The reasons vary. Some people may identify as Black because they do not feel connected to the American state. Others may identify as Black because they do not identify with the African continent. There are various historical, social and political reasons why one might prefer to identify as Black. The term has historically connected people of African descent around the world and was revived during the Black Power Movement.

4 Why do some people prefer African American?

Jesse Jackson popularized the term, which had already existed, in the 1980s. It mirrors hyphenated names for other American groups. Some people may identify themselves as African American to resist Black as a socially constructed category. Others may identify this way to assert their American identity. There are many reasons one might identify as African American.

5 How do multiracial people identify or fit in?

This varies from person to person and can change as a person ages. Many multiracial people struggle with this because society categorizes people by race, and multiracial people fit into more than one category. The U.S. Census Bureau began letting people check more than one race in 2000. In general, finding one's place usually depends upon environment and experience. A multiracial person raised where one race is predominant might identify more with that community. This can lead them to authenticity questions about other parts of their identity.

6 What is the African diaspora?

The African diaspora is a byproduct of the Trans-Atlantic slave trade, which dispersed millions of people. The Trans-Atlantic Slave Trade Database estimates that 12.5 million Africans were taken to the Americas and the Caribbean. About 1.8 million died en route. This forced move imposed a negative legacy. Overlaying new locations on African origins changed identities.

7 What is the Great Migration?

This was a post-Reconstruction move within the United States from the South to the North. From about 1916 to 1970, some six million African Americans moved out of the rural South to cities in the Northeast, Midwest and West. People fled lynchings and other forms of violence and segregation. They sought opportunity. After moving, they faced some of the same issues and met new forms of segregation in housing, education, employment and more.

8 Are there differences among Black groups in the United States?

Yes. African-American, African immigrant and Afro-Caribbean people have their own national and geographic contexts and legacies of colonialism, enslavement or migration. Black Caribbeans began migrating to the United States, oftentimes New York City, in the first half of the 1900s. Africans began migrating to the United States after the Civil Rights Movement. Differences can be linguistic, cultural, religious, political, historical and more. While different, they might feel connected through a collective Black or Pan-African identity.

9 What are Pan-Africanism and the Pan-African flag?

Pan-Africanism is a combination of political ideologies. It stresses the shared origins, economic and social interests held by people of African descent. A basic goal is to unify people worldwide through their African origins and culture. Pan-African unity is seen as essential to economic, political and social progress. The movement goes back to at least the mid 19th century and has roots in Africa, Europe and the Americas. Dr. W.E.B. DuBois convened a Pan-African Congress in 1919 in Paris. According to the Pan-African Alliance, Marcus Garvey's Universal Negro Improvement Association is credited with creating the Pan-African flag in 1920. The flag has horizontal red, black and green stripes. Red represents the blood that links all Black people. Black represents their shared ancestral past. Green represents the unification of Africa. Pan-Africanism has also been represented by green, yellow and red.

10 What is the Negro National Anthem?

This began as the 1899 poem *Lift Ev'ry Voice and Sing* by James Weldon Johnson. Set to music by Johnson's brother, J. Rosamond Johnson, this became known as the Negro National Anthem or Hymn. It was presented on Feb. 12, 1900, in Jacksonville, Florida, by 500 schoolchildren at a celebration of Abraham Lincoln's birthday. The National Association for the Advancement of Colored People adopted *Lift Ev'ry Voice and Sing* as its official song. The song represents the resilience and strength of Black people. It begins:

> *Lift ev'ry voice and sing,*
> *Till earth and heaven ring.*
> *Ring with the harmonies of Liberty;*
> *Let our rejoicing rise ..."*

Audio used courtesy Keith Hampton, artistic director/ founder, and the Chicago Community Chorus.

Listen to the audio at: http://bit.ly/1P8aeo2

History

11 How long did slavery last in the United States?

Slavery existed since before the U.S. Constitution was ratified in 1789. The Spanish brought African slaves to the New World in the 1500s. The British brought 20 to Jamestown, Virginia, in 1619. The 13th Amendment to the Constitution abolished slavery in 1865. But it contained this exception: "Neither slavery nor involuntary servitude, except as a punishment for crime whereof the party shall have been duly convicted, shall exist within the United States, or any place subject to their jurisdiction." Exploitation maintained free or cheap labor and led to convict leasing and debt peonage. Black people were forced to work off so-called debts or because of alleged crimes. Black codes, Jim Crow laws and other programs and systems held African Americans at second-class status.

12 What is the Emancipation Proclamation and what did it do?

In 1863, Lincoln issued a proclamation and executive order encouraging slaves in the South to become contrabands behind Union lines. It applied only in areas of the 10 Southern states that had seceded from the union. Those areas did not recognize his authority. States that had seceded in all or in part were Alabama, Arkansas, Florida,

Georgia, Louisiana, Mississippi, North Carolina, South Carolina, Texas and Virginia. Lincoln's proclamation did not address slavery in Union border states. Lincoln's action tied slavery to preserving the union, the major issue in the Civil War. The proclamation set the stage for the 13th Amendment, but it did not end slavery. Some celebrate the end of slavery on Juneteenth, short for June 19th. On that day in 1865, two months after the Civil War, Union troops arrived in Galveston to take control of Texas and enforce the Emancipation Proclamation.

13 Why does slavery have such a lasting effect?

Slavery remains an issue because current inequities are rooted in it. For many, slavery's effects are manifested daily. It is echoed through limits on occupational mobility, income and wealth, property ownership, equitable education, the political process and higher rates of imprisonment. Some argue that multi-generational trauma has caused post-traumatic slavery syndrome.

14 What are reparations?

Reparations are made to right past wrongs. They are often payments. The United States has paid more than $1.5 billion to settle claims made by Black farmers in a class-action lawsuit against the U.S. Department of Agriculture. The case was called Pigford v. Glickman. It was about discrimination in farm loans and assistance paid between 1981 and 1996. In 1989, U.S. Rep. John Conyers (D-Detroit) began introducing bills to create a commission to study more sweeping reparations for events dating back to slavery. Those bills have not advanced. Japanese Americans interned during World War II have received $1.6 billion in reparations and a formal apology from the U.S. government. Native Americans have received several payments including a $3.4 billion settlement in 2012.

15 What does "separate but equal" mean?

The 14th Amendment to the Constitution, ratified in 1868, called for equal treatment under the law. In 1892, a Black man named Homer Plessy was arrested for sitting in a train car designated for Whites. His case, Plessy v. Ferguson, went to the U.S. Supreme Court. The court ruled that as long as facilities were equal, segregation was constitutional. Jim Crow laws, named after a derogatory minstrel show character, began when Reconstruction ended in 1877. While the laws maintained separate services, they were often not equal.

16 What did Jim Crow laws do?

Jim Crow laws enforced strict segregation between Black and White people. The laws were enforced primarily in the South and were used to justify segregation for almost 80 years. They restricted African Americans' access to businesses and public amenities including schools, transportation, housing, retail and restaurants, bathrooms, drinking fountains and more. These laws discouraged interaction between the races, and often cast Black people as second-class citizens. Many resisted Jim Crow laws. One was 15-year-old Claudette Colvin, who in March, 1955, refused to give up her seat to a White man and move to the back of the bus in Montgomery, Alabama. Colvin was arrested. Nine months later, Rosa Parks was arrested for doing that, too.

17 What is Brown v. the Board of Education?

In the early 1950s, a number of lawsuits challenged school segregation. Five were consolidated as Brown v. The Board of Education of Topeka. This became the premier case against school segregation and went before the U.S. Supreme Court. Thurgood Marshall and a team of NAACP attorneys argued that unequal schooling treated Black children as though they were inferior to White children. The court ruled unanimously in 1954 that the 58-year-old "separate but equal" doctrine was unconstitutional.

18 Did the ruling desegregate schools?

Although the ruling ended Jim Crow laws, school segregation did not end immediately. In 1955, plans were made to desegregate schools. In 1957, the U.S. government sent troops to enforce the ruling and to protect the "Little Rock Nine," African-American students who had registered for a previously all-White high school in Arkansas. Later, people firebombed and shot at buses used to integrate schools. According to the nonprofit Economic Policy Institute and others, schools have resegregated.

19 When was the Civil Rights Movement?

The U.S. Congress passed four civil rights acts between 1866 and 1875, but inequities continued and pressure built for more action. Brown v. The Board of Education has been described as the start of the modern Civil Rights Movement. Its method was nonviolent civil disobedience. In the 1960s, nonviolent protesters held sit-ins throughout the South at segregated restaurants, lunch counters and stores. The first sit-in was held on Feb. 1, 1960, when four North Carolina A&T students refused to leave a Greensboro Woolworth's convenience store. The movement continued until the passage of the Civil Rights Act of 1964 and the Voting Rights Act of 1965. Civil rights activism continues in demonstrations and in social media.

20 What were the successes of the movement?

The federal government adopted laws addressing equality in education, housing and voting. Those laws have since been curtailed. The 2013 U.S. Supreme Court decision in Shelby County v. Holder let states pass more restrictive voting laws. That has meant reduced voting hours, barriers to voter registration and requirement of government identification to vote. A 2015 poll by CBS found that 54 percent of Americans and 72 percent of African Americans felt that none or only some goals of the Civil Rights Movement had been achieved.

21 What is affirmative action?

In the United States, affirmative action began under the Civil Rights Act of 1964. It was a way to address discrimination based on gender and race. Other countries also have affirmative action policies. Rulings expanded the U.S. law to include disability, ethnic origin and age. Affirmative action is used in employment, education, government contracts and more. Since 2000, several suits have been brought challenging the racial dimensions of U.S. affirmative action. One myth is that African Americans are the chief beneficiaries of affirmative action. That is not true.

The U.S. Department of Labor has said that White women have been the primary beneficiaries of affirmative action policies.

22 What is "reverse discrimination" or "reverse racism?"

These phrases are used in lawsuits and in accusations that affirmative action puts men and non-minorities at a disadvantage for college admission, scholarships and jobs. Research shows that this scarcely happens. A 1995 Brandeis University study of 3,000 discrimination suits found that about 100 had charged reverse discrimination. The courts ordered relief in six of those cases.

23 What is Black History Month?

The idea had its origins in 1915. Harvard PhD Carter G. Woodson and others established the Association for the Study of Negro Life and History. A year later, the group started the Journal of Negro History. In 1926, Woodson created Negro History Week to bring attention to history that was not in school curricula. U.S. presidents have annually recognized February as Black History Month starting with Gerald R. Ford in 1976. The United Kingdom and Canada observe it, as well. Black History Month has been controversial. Some say that designating just one month for Black history confines and diminishes it during the rest of the year. Others call it unnecessary special treatment.

24 What is Kwanzaa?

Kwanzaa is a celebration of African heritage and principles. It occurs Dec. 26 through Jan. 1. It grew out of the Black Nationalist Movement in the mid 1960s. Kwanzaa was created by Dr. Maulana Karenga, chairman of Black Studies at California State University. From the Swahili phrase "first fruits of the harvest," Kwanzaa celebrates seven principles, which are also identified in that East African language. They are:

- **umoja**   unity
- **kujichagulia**   self-determination
- **ujima**   collective responsibility
- **ujamaa**   cooperative economics
- **nia**   purpose
- **kuumba**   creativity
- **imani**   faith

Kwanzaa also has seven symbols. They are fruits, vegetables or nuts; a mat; a candleholder; seven candles (three red, three green and one black); corn; gifts and a communal cup signifying unity. Kwanzaa was intended to be independent of religion, though some families celebrate Kwanzaa with religious holidays.

Language

25 What is Ebonics?

Dr. Geneva Smitherman identifies African American Language, or Ebonics, as a system of "Africanized semantic, grammatical, pronunciation, and rhetorical patterns" unique to the Black community. Smitherman is a sociolinguist and Black studies scholar at Michigan State University. Universally embraced words, phrases, and actions such as the "high-five" come from Black language and cultural practices.

26 Why is it OK for Black people, but not White people, to use the n-word?

Many scholars theorize that the n-word is flipped, a feature of Black communication called semantic inversion. Inversion happens when African American Language speakers use a Standard American English word or phrase to mean its opposite. Vernacular speakers flip the definition of the n-word from negative to positive to reclaim power and self-identification. Some scholars argue the n-word is attached to race-based oppression, which they refer to as a cultural tax. White people, not having experienced this oppression, are not entitled to use the n-word that way. African Americans generally agree it is not OK for White people to use the n-word. Many people, Black and White, condemn its use by anyone. Some Black youth and others in the Hip-Hop Nation applaud it.

27 What are some features of Black communication styles?

Inversion, as just described, created the now popular and crossover use of "bad" to mean "good." Call-response, described in the next answer, is another feature of Black communication. Another is the use of "be" in the syntax (grammar) of the language. "Be" is part of what Georgetown University linguist and professor Dr. Ralph Fasold deems a "powerful system for specifying verbal relationships" in African American Language. One example is using "be" to convey the character or nature of a reality, event or action over time. Thus, a Black speaker might say "The coffee be cold." This does not mean and cannot be translated into Standard English as "The coffee is cold." In fact, at the time the speaker is making this statement, the coffee in question may very well be hot. Fasold talks about a sign in the window of a bar in Seattle: "We be non-smoking." He called this a blundering attempt to use African American Language, undoubtedly to ridicule the language and its speakers. The sign does not mean that the bar is non-smoking. On the contrary. In the vernacular, "We be non-smoking" means that sometimes it is and sometimes it isn't a non-smoking bar. Hence, a patron looking for a non-smoking bar would not know when, on what days, at what times, the bar is non-smoking.

28 Are Black people loud?

Not necessarily. It depends on the context and the expectations in that space. All people are more likely to be loud and speak with emotion when, for example, they're with friends rather than sitting alone. Additionally, in Black communication, there is a conversational style that some scholars refer to as call-response. This means that whoever is speaking issues a "call" and expects listeners to respond, verbally and nonverbally. Responding shows one is getting the message and is in tune with the speaker. This is similar to the style in the traditional Black Church, where the pastor and congregation call and respond throughout the sermon and service. The congregation's responses are not interruptions, but support. They help reinforce the message and drive it home. For those unfamiliar with Black linguistic practices, call-response can seem loud.

29 What is code switching?

Code switching is changing the way one speaks depending on the situation at hand. Within the Black community, some people speak differently with their friends than they do with their family. Some African Americans may use Standard English at work and the vernacular in familiar Black spaces. When Black people code switch, they are adjusting their speaking style to fit into a social context and to accommodate the speakers in that space. Code switching is a learned skill. It does not happen automatically. Youth from families where African American Language is the dominant language will enter school speaking African American Language. By the same token, youth from families where Standard English is the dominant language will enter school speaking Standard English. For either group, to master code switching requires dedicated, well-trained teachers and long-term experience and exposure to linguistic varieties other than the home language.

30 How can it be offensive to compliment a Black person for being articulate?

When someone remarks that a Black person is articulate, it can imply that this is surprising behavior. This can be insulting for the individual or toward African Americans generally. So, this apparent compliment can meet a negative reaction. Because Standard American English is often seen as "proper" and spoken by White people, noting that someone speaks well can challenge Black identity. Authenticity issues arise when someone says that a Black person "talks White." This can happen among Black people, as well.

Families

31 How many Black households are headed by one parent?

According to a 2013 Census report, 55 percent of Black children lived in a one-parent home. Other rates were 31 percent for Hispanics, 20 percent for Whites and 13 percent for Asian Americans. American families are changing. According to a Pew analysis of Census data, fewer than half of all U.S. children under 18 live with two heterosexual parents in their first marriage. One can't guess an individual's family structure from their race and shouldn't make inferences based on type. One study found about 70 types of African-American family structures compared to about 40 types for White families. This can mean multiple generations, more distant relatives and unrelated people living under one roof.

32 Are African-American families larger than others?

African-American households are larger than the U.S. average, according to the Census Bureau. In 2014, the average African-American household was 3.48 members compared to a national average of 2.63 members.

33 How prevalent are multiracial marriages among African Americans?

The Pew Research Center found that in 2013, 25 percent of newlywed Black males and 12 percent of newlywed Black females married people of another race. This amounted to 19 percent of all Black newlyweds. Rates were 7 percent for White Americans and 28 percent for Asian Americans. A 2012 Pew study found that 26 percent of Hispanics married someone of a different ethnicity.

34 How prevalent are teen pregnancies among African Americans?

Black and Latina teens are about twice as likely as non-Hispanic White teens to become pregnant. According to the National Campaign to Prevent Teen and Unplanned Pregnancy, in 2014 the rate for Hispanic teens was 38 percent and the rate for non-Hispanic Black teens was 35 percent. The rate for non-Hispanic White teens was 17 percent. Rates for all groups are falling. Black and Latina pregnancy rates are falling faster than the rate for White teens. The Pew Charitable Trusts cites poverty, lack of education and less access to contraceptives as factors in teen pregnancy.

35 Are there African-American traditions for naming children?

There are several, as there are with other groups. Many Black families follow widespread U.S. practices, naming children after relatives, people they admire or figures from their religion. Historically, there has also been a backlash against names imposed during slavery. Researchers say a shift during the Black Power Movement of the 1960s prompted some parents to choose African names. Names are also chosen or invented for their uniqueness or to confer status. Several studies have shown bias for or against job candidates on the basis of race or ethnicity inferred from names.

Religion

36 How important is religion to African Americans?

African Americans report religious affiliation more frequently than the general U.S. population. They also place greater importance on religion in their lives. The Pew Research Center found in late 2015 that 75 percent of Black Americans said religion was "very important" to them. The next closest group was Hispanic people at 59 percent. African Americans were also most likely to pray, participate in worship, read scriptures, believe in God and view religion as a source of guidance.

37 What religions do African Americans follow?

According to the Pew Research Center, 51 percent of the U.S. population overall affiliates with Protestantism. Fifty-nine percent of African Americans affiliate with historically Black Protestant churches. Historically Black churches include Baptist, Methodist, Pentecostal, Holiness and Non-denominational, among others. Fifteen percent of African Americans identified with Evangelical Protestant churches including Baptist, Non-denominational, Pentecostal and Restorationist. Twelve percent were unaffiliated, meaning they reported they were atheist, agnostic or nothing in particular. Four percent of African Americans identify

African American Religious Affiliation Compared to U.S. Population

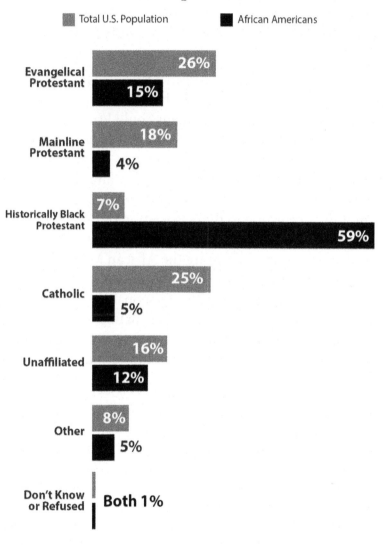

Total U.S. Population   African Americans

Evangelical Protestant
- 26%
- 15%

Mainline Protestant
- 18%
- 4%

Historically Black Protestant
- 7%
- 59%

Catholic
- 25%
- 5%

Unaffiliated
- 16%
- 12%

Other
- 8%
- 5%

Don't Know or Refused
- Both 1%

Illustration: Madeline Carino
Source: U.S. Census Bureau

with mainline Protestant churches. Five percent identify as Catholic and another 5 percent identify as something else. One percent of African Americans identify as Muslim. They comprise about a quarter of all American Muslims, who are about 1 percent of the nation's total population.

38 What is the Black Church?

Since slavery, the Black Church has been a source of sanctuary and strength. It has been a resource for freedom, education, jobs and support. The church was one of the few places where African Americans could lead. From this foundation, churches became meeting places during the Civil Rights Movement. The importance of Black churches has made them targets for arson and other attacks. These still go on and represent assaults on the heart of the Black community. According to the Association of Religion Data Archives, the Black Church "has been composed of seven major denominations." They are the African Methodist Episcopal Church, the African Methodist Episcopal Zion Church, the Christian Methodist Episcopal Church, the Church of God in Christ, the National Baptist Convention of America, the National Baptist Convention, USA, Inc., and the Progressive National Baptist Convention, Inc.

Race Relations

39 How are race relations in America?

A 2015 New York Times/CBS News poll showed that almost 60 percent of Americans said race relations were generally bad. This was more negative than when President Barack Obama was elected. Black respondents were more likely than White respondents to say relations are bad. The survey was conducted one month after a White supremacist killed nine Black churchgoers in South Carolina. That followed a series of videos showing shootings and brutal treatment of Black citizens by White police officers.

40 How are relations between police and the Black community?

The study just mentioned found a similar disparity in police-community relations. Black and White respondents were asked whether police made them feel safe or anxious. This is how they responded:

	Safe	Anxious
Black	58%	37%
White	82%	17%

A number of high-profile incidents in which police killed or violently subdued African Americans have worsened relations, which have historically been strained.

41 What is institutional racism?

Institutional racism is when policies and practices put people who are not of the dominant race at a disadvantage. This happens in government, business, education at all levels, news and entertainment media and other systems. Housing policies that turn away single parents, parents with more children or people with lower incomes can be forms of institutional racism. Hiring and promotion patterns can reflect institutional racism. It was a factor in a wave of protests on college campuses that began in 2015. School discipline systems that disproportionately send Black students into the criminal justice system have been called "the school-to-prison pipeline." When people say an institution is racist, they may not be referring to intent, but to the structures and policies of the institution.

42 What is systemic racism?

This term describes social values that support personal and institutional discrimination. As a social concept, systemic racism explains how people of color must adapt to a society not built for them, while White people readily fit in.

43 What is White privilege?

White privilege refers to advantages for people with white skin. This includes advantages they might not even know about. It can be a product of systemic racism. Advantages can be economic, social or educational. One kind of privilege is freedom from barriers, suspicions or expectations that non-White people experience daily. Another can be freedom from judgment or denial surrounding success or aspirations. For example, if two people acquire the same job or car, the White person's success might be taken for granted while the Black person is asked how he or she managed it.

44 What does "colorblind" mean?

In his 1896 opposition to the separate-but-equal 14th Amendment, Supreme Court Justice John Marshal Harlan wrote, "Our Constitution is color-blind." Today, colorblindness is the ideal or hope that people will not be treated or judged by their race. This is difficult to achieve. Additionally, some want racial identities and experiences to be recognized, understood and valued. Colorblindness is similar to the broader idea that the United States moved past racial disparity when Barack Obama was elected president. Events say otherwise.

45 Can Black people be prejudiced?

No race is free of bias and prejudice. People can be biased against people of other races and against people of their own race. Discussions about bias, prejudice and racism often turn on how those terms are interpreted. A good starting point for such discussions is an agreement on what they mean.

46 Do African Americans isolate themselves socially?

People of all racial and ethnic groups sometimes congregate. It might be for support and a shared familiarity and culture. When people cluster, it is generally with the intention of being together, not keeping others away. It is also more noticeable when smaller groups do this within a larger group, which might be doing the same thing. A book, "Why are All the Black Kids Sitting Together in the Cafeteria?" is listed with the resources at the end of this guide.

47 What does it mean to "play the race card?"

To say someone is "playing the race card," is to say they are injecting race into a discussion. To say someone is doing this can be an attempt to deflect, diminish or discredit race's effects. Black feminist scholar bell hooks writes that the expression "trivializes discussions of racism, implying it's all just a game." She calls this a backlash against talk about race, "more often than not representing it as mere hysteria."

Demographics

48 What percentage of the U.S. population is Black?

As of 2014, there were approximately 42 million Black citizens in the United States. That's about 13 percent of the U.S. population. Black people were the largest minority group in the United States until 2001, when Hispanics surpassed them. These designations overlap because one is racial and the other is cultural. The 2010 U.S. Census reported that about 2.5 million of the nation's 54 million Hispanics were Black. Gallup polls say people typically overestimate the percentages of the population that is Black or Hispanic.

49 How is the African-American population distributed?

According to the U.S. Census Bureau, 55 percent of the Black population is concentrated in the southern United States. Sixty percent live in 10 states. The states with the highest African-American populations are New York, Florida and Texas.

2015 Population Estimate

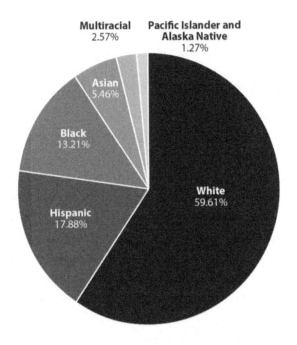

Projections are for Hispanic people and non-Hispanic people of various races. The Census Bureau predicts declines in the percentage of Americans who are Black and White and that by 2045 there will be no majority group in the U.S.

Illustrations: Madeline Carino
Source: U.S. Census Bureau

2025 Projection

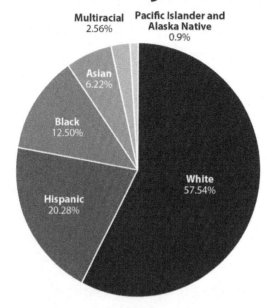

Multiracial
2.56%

Pacific Islander and
Alaska Native
0.9%

Asian
6.22%

Black
12.50%

White
57.54%

Hispanic
20.28%

2045 Projection

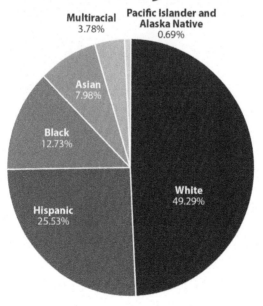

Multiracial
3.78%

Pacific Islander and
Alaska Native
0.69%

Asian
7.98%

Black
12.73%

White
49.29%

Hispanic
25.53%

Where do African Americans live?

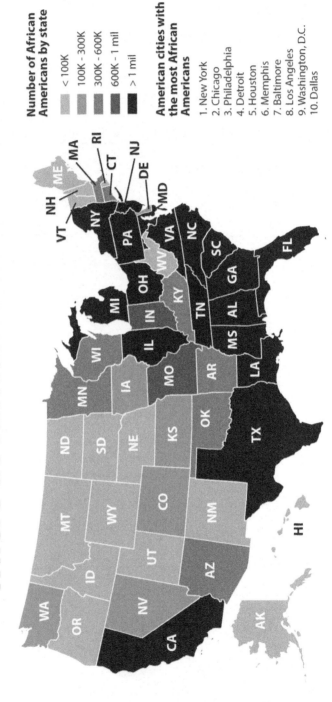

Number of African Americans by state

- < 100K
- 100K - 300K
- 300K - 600K
- 600K - 1 mil
- > 1 mil

American cities with the most African Americans

1. New York
2. Chicago
3. Philadelphia
4. Detroit
5. Houston
6. Memphis
7. Baltimore
8. Los Angeles
9. Washington, D.C.
10. Dallas

Illustration: Madeline Carino
Source: U.S. Census Bureau

50 How are populations distributed at the local level?

A history of housing laws and policies has caused residential segregation and clustered African Americans in cities. Policies have included red lining and deed restrictions that confined African Americans to certain neighborhoods and substandard housing. There have also been restrictive or exploitative mortgage policies, foreclosures, steering and even confiscation of property. This has affected a host of related issues including health, wealth, education and access to work. Recently, Black people have been moving out of cities. Census data show a decline in the proportion of African Americans living in the largest city in all 20 of the country's largest metropolitan areas. Black people are moving to the South and to suburbs for greater opportunities or safety and because of rising prices in gentrified urban areas.

Education

51 How do African Americans' educational levels compare with others'?

According to the National Center for Education Statistics, high school graduation rates for Black students are lower than for most other groups. However, they are rising faster. These were education levels reported in 2014 for 25- to 29-year-olds:

	Completed high school	Bachelor's degree
Asian Americans	97%	61%
White Americans	96%	41%
African Americans	92%	22%
Hispanics	75%	15%

Several factors affect education. For generations, laws and residency limited African Americans to lower performing schools. This and lower income limited access to college.

52 What are Historically Black Colleges and Universities?

HBCUs, as they are called, are colleges and universities created with the mission of educating Black students. They were established in response to policies that excluded Black students from institutions of higher education. There are

103 HBCUs in the United States. They accept people of all races.

53 What is the role of Black fraternities and sororities?

Black fraternities and sororities were established as civic action groups. They were founded at Black and majority White universities. They worked to advance their schools during a time of segregation and oppression. These nine organizations, known as the Divine Nine, were unified by the National Pan-Hellenic Council starting in 1930. Their mission is progress for all Black people.

The Divine Nine, with their year and place of founding and entrance into the Council:

- Alpha Phi Alpha Fraternity, 1906, Cornell University, entered in 1931
- Alpha Kappa Alpha Sorority, 1908, Howard University, entered in 1930
- Kappa Alpha Psi Fraternity, 1911, Indiana University, entered in 1930
- Omega Psi Phi Fraternity, 1911, Howard University, entered in 1930
- Delta Sigma Theta Sorority, 1913, Howard University, entered in 1930
- Phi Beta Sigma Fraternity, 1914, Howard University, entered in 1931
- Zeta Phi Beta Sorority, 1920, Howard University, entered in 1930
- Sigma Gamma Rho Sorority, 1922, Butler University, entered in 1937
- Iota Phi Theta Fraternity, 1963, Morgan State University, entered in 1997

View video at: http://bit.ly/1OZAxCZ

Wealth, Work and Money

54 What is average income for African Americans?

A 2015 U.S. Census report showed median income in 2014 was $35,398 for Black households compared to $53,657 for all households. Income for all groups was lower in 2014 than it had been in 2007, but the decline had been steeper for Black families. In 2014, Black household income was 59 percent of what White households made. Black men made 70 cents for each dollar earned by White men. Black women, on average, earned 77 cents for every dollar earned by White women, according to Census reports. Income is affected by wages, education, occupational mobility, health and other factors. These are influenced by inequities in housing and other forms of structural racism. According to the Census Bureau, the 2014 poverty rate was 26.2 percent for African Americans, 23.6 percent for Hispanics of all races, 12 percent for Asians and 10.1 percent for Whites. The proportion of children in poverty is greater in every group, according to the Annie E. Casey Foundation's Kids Count data center. It showed these percentages for children living in poverty in 2014:

African American	38 percent
Native American	37 percent
Hispanic	32 percent

| Asian American | 14 percent |
| White | 13 percent |

11 THOUSAND DOLLARS

View video at: http://bit.ly/1J1hg1U

55 How does wealth compare among races?

First, think of wealth as lifetime savings, not just income, which is money coming in every year. The Urban Institute reported Black families had accumulated an average of $11,000 in 2013, compared to $13,700 for Hispanic families and $134,200 for White families. White families currently have 12 times more wealth than Black families. The wealth gap nearly doubled between 1995 and 2013. Lower wages hinder wealth accumulation. Education can increase income and wealth, but student loan debt contributes to the wealth gap. Black families on average must borrow more money for someone to attend college, and degrees are less likely to lead to jobs. Black people are also less likely to own their own homes or have retirement savings, which are prime creators of inherited wealth.

56 How does African-American unemployment compare with other groups?

According to the U.S. Bureau of Labor Statistics, in late 2015, unemployment rates for people 16 and older were 9.5 percent for African Americans, 6.5 percent for Hispanics, 4.5 percent for Whites and 3.7 percent for Asian Americans. This has been a consistent pattern. The rate reflects the proportion of people looking for jobs. People who have stopped looking are not counted. The Economic Policy Institute says one reason for higher Black unemployment is that African Americans look for work longer than others do. Employment equity relies on a number of factors including place of residence, income, education and access to transportation.

57 Does most government food assistance go to African Americans?

African Americans were 25.7 percent of the nation's 15.7 million Supplemental Nutrition Assistance Program recipients in 2013. According to the U.S. Department of Agriculture, 40.2 percent were White. Hispanic people of all races comprised 10.3 percent and Asian Americans comprised 2.1 percent. Race was unknown for 12.8 percent. The proportion of Black recipients is about twice their share of the population, but most African Americans are not on food assistance.

58 Is the Black community the major recipient of other government aid?

There are several kinds of aid and they are based on income, not race. Because African Americans are more likely to be living in poverty, they are more likely to be in safety net welfare programs. In 2012, 39.8 percent of recipients were Black, 38.8 percent were White, 15.7 percent were Hispanic, 2.4 percent were Asian American and 3.3 percent were described as other. More government aid comes as tax breaks on mortgage interest, property taxes and some investments. According to the Congressional Budget Office, about two-thirds of government aid for homeownership and retirement goes to the richest 20 percent of taxpayers.

59 How digitally connected are African Americans?

Mobile devices have narrowed the digital divide. A 2014 Pew Research report of Black and White consumers showed identical rates of smartphone and cellphone ownership in the 18-29 age group. In terms of platforms, 40 percent of African Americans use Twitter, compared to 28 percent of White Americans in that age group. "Black Twitter" is a major connector. Older African Americans are less likely to have Internet access at home, but mobile access compensates.

Health

60 How does African-American life expectancy compare with others?

Average life expectancy in 2013 was 75.5 years for Black babies and 79.1 for White babies. The gap had narrowed from 5.9 years in 1999 to 3.6 years in 2013. A report in late 2015 by the Centers for Disease Control and Prevention cited several reasons. The biggest was a greater decline in heart disease deaths for African Americans. Black people also had greater declines in deaths due to cancer, HIV, unintentional injuries and health problems during infancy.

61 Are life expectancies the same everywhere?

The Social Science Research Council's 2013-2014 Measure of America report showed that life expectancies vary by state. For example, the average life expectancy for African Americans is age 72.2 years in Arkansas and 79.7 in Minnesota.

62 What is the infant mortality rate for Black babies?

Infant mortality is the death of a baby within the first 12 months. The rate for all U.S. babies in 2010 was 6.1 per

1,000 live births. The rate for babies born to Black mothers was almost double, at 11.4. The Centers for Disease Control and Prevention reports that the survival rates for African-American babies have been improving faster than rates for other groups.

63 What are the leading causes of death for African Americans?

The top three causes of death for Black and White Americans are the same, according to the Centers for Disease Control and Prevention. They are heart disease, cancer and stroke. The next leading causes of death for African Americans are diabetes, unintentional accidents, homicide, HIV/AIDS, respiratory disease, kidney conditions and blood poisoning.

64 Are some medical conditions more prevalent among African Americans?

Diabetes, hypertension, obesity and heart disease are more common among African Americans than others, according to the Centers for Disease Control and Prevention. Causes tend to be environmental and social rather than genetic. Medical anthropologist Clarence C. Gravlee suggests that understanding how race is culturally constructed helps explain racism's biological consequences.

65 Can racism cause health problems?

Scientists say racism harms health in two ways. According to the National Institutes for Health, racial discrimination can directly hurt mental, physical and social health. Researchers call this race-based traumatic stress injury.

Indirectly, racism also harms environmental factors such as living standards, housing, mobility, and access to health resources and healthy food.

66 Can subtle racism be harmful, too?

Slights and snubs are called racial microaggressions. Some are unintentional. Microaggressions can be questions or expressions about a person's identity or abilities. They can be behaviors. Racial microaggressions include judgments like "You don't act like a normal Black person," and "You probably can't afford that." They can be actions like locking the car door when a person perceived as a threat walks by. There is evidence these experiences pile up and can hurt mental health and performance at work or school. The term microaggression has been around since the 1970s. According to Columbia University's Dr. Derald Wing Sue, there have been 5,500 microaggression studies since 2005.

67 Is sickle cell disease a Black condition?

Sickle cell trait is genetic, not racial. Some genetic disorders can be traced to certain geographic areas. Sickle cell disease occurs in approximately one out of every 315 African-American births, according to the National Heart, Lung and Blood Institute. The trait can lead to the disease in which red blood cells are sickle shaped, rather than rounded, and interfere with the body's ability to distribute oxygen. The trait occurs among people with ancestry from areas where malaria is more common. According to the American Society of Hematology, "Sickle cell trait can also affect Hispanics, South Asians, Caucasians from southern Europe, and people from Middle Eastern countries."

68 Is there a health insurance gap for African Americans?

Yes, but it is closing, according to a 2015 U.S. Health and Human Services report. It said the number of Black people without insurance declined from 24.6 percent in 2013 to 15.9 percent in the first half of 2014. The proportion of uninsured Hispanic people declined from 40.3 percent to 33.2 percent. The rate for White people without insurance declined from 14.0 percent to 11.1 percent.

Gender and Sex

69 Where do sexual stereotypes about African Americans come from?

These have been around since slavery began. Early stereotypes portrayed Black people as less civilized. Sexual stereotypes then reinforced distinctions of cultural superiority and inferiority. Early sexual stereotypes cast Black women as targets for assault and Black men as predators. In 1955, 14-year-old Emmett Till was kidnapped from his uncle's home and beaten to death in Mississippi for reportedly flirting with a White woman. His killers' acquittal by an all-White jury was seen as a reflection of stereotypes about Black male sexuality and Jim Crow segregation. The case helped prompt the modern Civil Rights Movement. Some sexual stereotypes are perpetuated today in pop culture.

70 How do issues of race and gender affect Black women?

As members of two historically marginalized groups, Black women face racism and sexism at the same time. UCLA professor Kimberlé Crenshaw coined the term "intersectionality" for this. She wrote that race is not often considered when looking at gender. Considering factors together helps explain discrimination that is not just race or gender specific. For example, Black women face challenges not experienced by Black men.

71 How does feminism regard Black women?

Historically, mainstream feminism has excluded and ignored Black women. The divide became apparent during the suffragist movement. After White women won the right to vote, most did not continue the fight for women of color. According to the national Black feminist Combahee River Collective, founded in 1973, "A Black feminist presence has evolved most obviously in connection with the second wave of the American women's movement beginning in the late 1960s. Black, other Third World, and working women have been involved in the feminist movement from its start, but both outside reactionary forces and racism and elitism within the movement itself have served to obscure our participation."

72 How does the Black community regard sexual orientation?

In a 2012 Gallup Poll, 4.6 percent of Black Americans identified as lesbian, gay, bisexual, or transgender. The Black Protestant Church has been less tolerant than other large Christian denominations, but a Pew Research Center report in late 2015 showed growing acceptance. The report said slightly more than half of Black Protestant Church members agreed that society should be more accepting of homosexuality. This compared to 39 percent approval in 2007. This was one of the biggest increases among U.S. Christian churches.

Appearance

73 Can you tell if people are African American by how they look?

Physical characteristics, called phenotypes, vary widely. Phenotypes are not good indicators of a person's origins, nationality, heritage or whether a person is mixed race. Assuming identity on the basis of looks is not a good basis for judging someone or asking questions.

74 What is colorism?

Colorism occurs when someone with lighter skin is favored over someone with darker skin. Colorism occurs within all races, as all have varieties of skin tone and hair color. Although no longer common, the "brown paper bag test" was an example of this among African Americans. With that test, some lighter-skinned or "high yellow" African Americans would exclude people if their skin was darker than a brown paper bag.

75 What is "passing?"

This is when someone appears to be and identifies as a member of another race. Historically, some African Americans passed as White to avoid racial injustice. In his novel *Black Like Me*, White journalist John Howard Griffin underwent treatments to turn his skin black. He wrote about the discrimination he experienced when he appeared to be African American.

76 Can African Americans get sunburned or tanned?

African Americans can absolutely get sunburned or tanned. According to dermatologist Aletha Maybank in Ebony Magazine, African Americans have better sun protection and a decreased risk for skin cancer than Whites. Still, they do not have full coverage. The higher amount of melanin in the skin of African Americans can have a natural sun protection factor of as much as 13. That compares to a factor of 3-4 in people with white skin. With continual exposure to the sun, dark skin produces more melanin and darkens. African Americans also can have sunstroke. They develop skin cancer at very low rates compared to White people. However, Black skin cancer patients have lower survival rates than White patients.

77 What is "ashy" skin?

Perhaps the most important aspect of African-American skin care is moisturizing to prevent "ashiness." This is just dry skin. It appears to be chalky or flaky on darker complexions. Everyone gets dry skin, and we all experience it more in dry weather. It is just not as noticeable on lighter skin. Ashiness shows up most on knees, elbows, arms and feet. Historically, ashiness was often associated with being poor or dirty, which may have contributed to the importance of Black skin care.

78 Can Black hairstyles be political?

They can be. People might wear their hair to suit their style sense, personality, history, comfort or convenience. Some people change their hair often. Black hairstyles have creative varieties from natural to straightened to curled and different kinds of braids. Black hair can be long or short, elaborate or shaved, and worn up or down. It can incorporate weaves, extensions and beads. Some people ask about hair to get to know more about the person.

View video at: http://bit.ly/1J1hgig

Culture and Contributions

79 Who are some major Black contributors to American literature?

Some names and titles are Maya Angelou, *"I Know Why the Caged Bird Sings;"* James Baldwin, *"The Fire Next Time;"* Langston Hughes, *"The Collected Poems of Langston Hughes;"* Zora Neale Hurston, *"Their Eyes Were Watching God;"* Audre Lord, *"The Black Unicorn;"* Toni Morrison, *"The Bluest Eye;"* and Richard Wright, *"Black Boy."*

80 What are African-American contributions to music?

Black musicians and composers have played a major role in shaping modern American music. Drawing on African traditions, people developed music through slavery, in churches, in the field and in factories. Black music includes gospel and spirituals, ragtime, country, blues, jazz, soul and, more recently, rap and hip-hop. Black music has inspired several major musical genres including folk, rock 'n' roll and pop. Black music continues to evolve and to spin off sub-genres.

81 What was the "Chitlin' Circuit?"

The "Chitlin' Circuit" was a touring route Black entertainers used in the early 20th century. It provided safe venues and reliable lodging for traveling performers during Jim Crow discrimination. From the 1930s into the 1950s, new types of music developed along the circuit. Some emerged from string bands. New genres included the blues and rock 'n' roll. Performers included Muddy Waters, B.B. King, Ruth Brow, Ray Charles, Aretha Franklin, Billie Holiday, James Brown and Lena Horne. The circuit also featured dance and comedy. Besides giving performers a stage, the circuit also helped support Black businesses. The circuit was named after boiled pig intestines, a soul-food staple. The name plays off Jewish entertainers' Borscht Belt.

82 What is hip-hop?

Hip-hop is often identified as just a music form, but it goes well beyond music. Originating in New York's South Bronx in the 1970s, hip-hop includes four elements: deejaying (also known as DJing or turntabling), MCing (emceeing or rapping), graffiti painting and breakdancing (B-boying). Hip-hop has been adapted by cultures around the world.

83 Why do some people assume African Americans are good dancers?

Dance was one of the few cultural dimensions early African Americans could bring from their homelands. Dancing celebrated milestones such as marriage or birth of a child. It expressed pride in heritage. Dancing also was a way to break into entertainment at a time when many employment fields were closed. Today, many popular dances come from the Black community. But we wouldn't assume that all African Americans can dance.

84 How often and accurately are African Americans represented in movies?

The Annenberg School for Communication & Journalism at the University of Southern California studies portrayal in movies. According to its 2013 study, minorities continue to be underrepresented and stereotyped in movies. Hollywood long produced blackface, starring White actors with painted faces, and films that exploited Black stereotypes. A 2015 report by the Ralph J. Bunche Center for African American Studies at UCLA agreed. In recent years, there has been a growing number of African-American directors, mostly men.

85 Are African Americans well represented in the news media?

Studies show that news media have historically underrepresented and misrepresented African Americans. According to the 1968 federal Kerner Commission report, "The media report and write from the standpoint of a white man's world. The ills of the ghetto, the difficulties of life there, the Negro's burning sense of grievance, are seldom conveyed." More recently, Harvard's Shorenstein Center reports, "Numerous studies documented the high rate at which persons of color were typically portrayed as violent or dangerous in newspapers and television." African Americans are also underrepresented in newsrooms. The American Society of News Editors reported in 2015 that the percentage of African Americans in newspaper and online newsrooms had fallen to 4.74 percent. This was the lowest since 2000. In 2014, the Radio Television Digital News Association reported that African-American representation was up from 10.2 percent to 10.7 percent at non-Hispanic stations.

86 What is the origin of African-American soul food?

African-American soul food dates back to slavery. It developed in the South. Soul food required creativity because it was based on using undesirable or leftover food products. Examples of soul food include collard, mustard and turnip greens, red beans and rice, lard, chitterlings and other less desirable parts of the pig. Once castoffs improvised into meals, soul food has spawned some upscale restaurants and its own cookbooks.

87 What are some creations of Black inventors?

Black inventors have made contributions in manufacturing, medicine, computing, chemistry and more. In the 1880s, Lewis Latimer improved Thomas A. Edison's electric light bulb so it would last more than a few days. In the early 1900s, Dr. Charles Drew revolutionized knowledge of plasma, leading to the creation of blood banks. Garrett Morgan invented the traffic signal and a modern-day gas mask. George Washington Carver invented thousands of uses for vegetables including peanuts. Patricia Bath, an ophthalmologist, invented a method for using lasers to treat cataracts. Shirley Jackson's developments in theoretical physics have led to advances in touch-tone telephones, caller ID, call waiting and fiber optics.

88 Why are there many Black athletes in some sports and not others?

Sports choices can largely be a result of exposure and opportunity. Sports have different degrees of availability. Golf can require greens fees and a lot of space. Hockey can require ice time and a lot of equipment. Basketball requires very little space and little equipment. Given exposure and opportunity, Black athletes have excelled at golf, hockey, tennis, skiing and swimming, sports not often associated with their race. Even in sports where African Americans are well represented, they are not as numerous in the coaches' office and owners' suites as in the locker rooms.

89 What are African-American military contributions?

The African-American proportion of the military exceeds the share in the overall population. African Americans have fought in the nation's wars from the beginning. Crispus Attucks, of Black and Native American ancestry, is regarded as the first casualty of the Revolutionary War. The Tuskegee Airmen, treated as an experiment in integration during World War II, had 1,000 Black pilots and 15,000 support personnel. The group was highly decorated and prompted moves to desegregate the military. African Americans are still underrepresented in the officer ranks, according to annual reports by USA Today.

90 What is cultural appropriation?

Cultural appropriation occurs in TV and movies, music, cartoons, Halloween costumes and language. It is when people use another group's cultural elements or artifacts in ways that can ridicule or be negative. Some see appropriation as an assault on culture. Cultural collaboration can lead to respectful sharing and fusion.

Criminal Justice

91 What is "mass incarceration?"

Mass incarceration is increased rates of imprisonment resulting from tougher penalties, especially for drug offenses. Arrests and mandatory minimum sentences have fueled this since the 1970s. During this period, African Americans have been locked up in numbers out of proportion with crime rates. According to the American Civil Liberties Union, "five times as many Whites are using drugs as African Americans, yet African Americans are sent to prison for drug offenses at 10 times the rate of Whites." Sentences are also longer. In 2013, the U.S. Sentencing Commission reported that sentences of Black men were almost 20 percent longer than sentences of White men convicted of similar crimes. According to the Southern Center for Social Justice, the number of women incarcerated has increased 800 percent over the past three decades. Black and Hispanic women have been imprisoned at greater rates than other women. In 2015, some politicians and law enforcement officials began calling for reforms and releases.

92 Is it true there are more Black men in prison than in college?

No, this is a myth. According to the Bureau of Justice Statistics, 526,000 Black men were in prison in 2013. That year, the National Center for Educational Statistics reported that 1,437,363 were enrolled in college. The myth has been used to illustrate high rates of imprisonment for Black men. According to the Bureau of Justice Statistics, Black males were imprisoned at rates 2.5 times greater than for Hispanic males and six times higher than for White males.

93 What are hate crimes?

Federal law says hate crimes are "motivated in whole or in part by an offender's bias against a race, religion, disability, ethnic origin or sexual orientation." According to an annual FBI report, 48.3 percent of hate crimes in 2014 were racially motivated. Of those, 62.7 percent stemmed from anti-Black sentiments. Another 22.7 percent stemmed from anti-White sentiments.

94 What are the statistics for Black-on-White homicides?

FBI statistics for 2014 show a prevalence of within-race violence, contrary to common perceptions. According to the FBI, 82 percent of the 3,021 White homicide victims were killed by White assailants. Fifteen percent were killed by Black assailants. For the nation's 2,451 Black homicide victims, 90 percent were killed by Black assailants. Eight percent were killed by White assailants. Northeastern University Criminology professor James Alan Fox has written that, "Because of the racial homogeneity of most neighborhoods . . . most stranger killings are" among people of the same race.

95 What is racial profiling?

Racial profiling means applying stereotypes to a group of people with negative consequences. Racial profiling can be subtle or direct. African Americans may find themselves followed by merchants in retail shops, treated differently in schools or restaurants, or pulled over more frequently than White drivers. Racial profiling also figures in "stop and frisk" cases. In those, police search individuals they suspect are involved in or are about to be involved in illegal activities. According to a 2013 Pew Research study, as many as 70 percent of Black respondents said police treat African Americans unfairly. Thirty-five percent said they experienced discrimination in the year before the study. Some Black parents give young children "the talk" about avoiding suspicion in stores. A similar talk tells new drivers how not to alarm police in a traffic stop. Other groups, notably Hispanics and Arab Americans, also get profiled by law enforcement and at borders.

Voting and Politics

96 Where do African Americans stand politically?

African Americans primarily vote Democratic. However, like any large group, this does not apply to everyone. Since 1964, an average of 88 percent of African Americans have voted Democratic. In the 2012 presidential election, about 95 percent of Black voters chose Barack Obama. African Americans from both major parties have held office at the local, state and national levels, though they are not represented in proportion to their share of the population.

97 What is voter turnout like for African Americans?

African-American voter turnout spiked in the 2008 and 2012 elections of President Barack Obama. Those rates were 69 percent and 67 percent, higher than the nation's average. Historically, the turnout of eligible Black voters has been lower than for eligible White voters but higher than for Hispanic and Asian-American voters.

98 What is the Voting Rights Act?

The 15th Amendment gave equal voting to all U.S. citizens in 1870, but discrimination against African Americans continued. Southern states used literacy tests and poll taxes to prevent African Americans from casting ballots. The Voting Rights Act, passed 95 years later in 1965, outlawed these practices. It allowed the federal government to oversee voting. In 2013, the U.S. Supreme Court struck down an important provision of the act. It ended the requirement that jurisdictions with discriminatory histories had to clear changes that could affect minority voters.

99 What is the NAACP?

This is the National Association for the Advancement of Colored People. It is a multiracial group of progressives from all political parties. It was founded on Feb. 12, 1909, the 100th anniversary of Lincoln's birth. Its mission is "to ensure the political, educational, social and economic equality of rights of all persons and to eliminate race-based discrimination." It has more than half a million members and supporters. The NAACP headquarters is in Baltimore. The organization has more than 2,000 branches and student chapters throughout the country and abroad. According to its website, the NAACP is "the nation's oldest, largest and most widely recognized grassroots-based civil rights organization."

100 What is the emphasis of #BlackLivesMatter?

According to its website, #BlackLivesMatter does not believe Black lives are more important than other lives. In fact, it says it stands with other oppressed peoples and views all lives as important. The campaign opposes police violence against Black people. While the group says all lives matter, not all lives face the same threats. According to Black Lives Matter, once Black people are free from oppression, the benefits will be wide reaching and transformative to society as a whole.

Epilogue

Our intention with this guide is not to separate people by focusing on differences, but to encourage conversation. A 2015 New York Times/CBS News poll showed that about two-thirds of White Americans said that none or just a few of the people they encounter every day are Black. Lack of exposure limits understanding. One person we interviewed for this guide said he wishes White people would drop qualifiers like, "My Black friend Terry" and say simply, "My friend Terry." We share his hope.

We invite you to watch or read the resources in the next section. More than that, we hope you talk with people you work with or live near. Get to know them as individuals. Hear them. These 100 questions and answers do not do justice to the variety of perspectives of millions of African Americans, who are as different as they are alike. We hope these 100 questions give rise to 1,000 new ones. Listen to the perspectives of several people, as no one can speak for an entire group.

In creating these guides, we have learned that while differences are very important, people share some core values. All people want to be safe, to be free, to be respected and to have a fair chance to succeed. By sharing perspectives and by understanding each other better, we believe that all lives can be enriched.

Books

Alexander, Michelle. *The New Jim Crow: Mass Incarceration in the Age of Colorblindness.* New York: The New Press. 2012.

Alim, H. Samy and Geneva Smitherman. *Articulate While Black: Barack Obama, Language, and Race in the U.S.* Oxford: Oxford University Press. 2012.

Asante, M.K. *Buck: A Memoir.* New York: Spiegel & Grau. 2014 reprint.

Coates, Ta-Nehisi. *Between the World and Me.* New York: Spiegel & Grau. 2015.

Collins, Patricia Hills. *Black Sexual Politics: African Americans, Gender, and the New Racism.* London: Routledge. 2005.

Dagbovie, Pero Gaglo. *What is African American History?* Champaign: University of Illinois Press. 2010.

Griffin, John Howard. *Black Like Me.* New York: Signet. 2010, 50th anniversary edition.

Harris, Jessica B. *High on the Hog: A Culinary Journey from Africa to America.* New York: Bloomsbury USA. 2012.

Hill, Marc Lamont. *Beats, Rhymes, and Classroom Life: Hip-Hop Pedagogy and the Politics of Identity.* New York: Teachers College Press. 2013.

hooks, bell. *Teaching Community: A Pedagogy of Hope.* London: Routledge. 2003.

hooks, bell. *We Real Cool: Black Men and Masculinity.* London: Routledge. 2003.

Karenga, Maulana. *Kwanzaa: A Celebration of Family, Community and Culture.* Los Angeles: University of Sankore Press. 2008.

Majors, Richard and Janet Mancini Billson. *Cool Pose: The Dilemmas of Black Manhood in America.* New York: Touchstone. 1993 reprint.

Paris, Peter. *The Social Teaching of the Black Churches.* Minneapolis: Augsburg Fortress Publishers. 1998.

Roth Jr., Lawrence C. *The Divine Nine: The History of African American Fraternities and Sororities.* New York: Kensington. 2001 reissue.

Smitherman, Geneva. *Talkin' That Talk: Language, Culture and Education in African America.* London: Routledge, 2000.

Smitherman, Geneva. *Word From the Mother: Language and African Americans.* London: Routledge, 2006.

Tatum, Beverly Daniel. *Why Are All the Black Kids Sitting Together in the Cafeteria? And Other Conversations About Race.* New York: Basic Books. 2003 revision.

Thomas, Ebony Elizabeth and Shanesa R.F. Brooks-Tatum (eds.) *Reading African American Experiences in the Obama Era: Theory, Advocacy and Activism.* Bern: Peter Lang Publishing, Inc. 2012.

Wilkerson, Isabel. *The Warmth of Other Suns: The Epic Story of America's Great Migration.* New York: New York: Vintage. 2011 reprint.

Videos

FOX. *12 Years a Slave.* 2013.

Grant, William R. (director). *Slavery and the Making of America.* Morgan Freeman narrates. Ambrose Studio. There is a companion book by the same title. 2005.

Lionsgate. Rock, Chris (co-producer, co-writer). *Good Hair: Sit Back and Relax.* 2009.

Mill Creek Entertainment. *Up from Slavery.* 2011.

PBS. *African American Lives.* 2006.

PBS. *The African Americans: Many Rivers to Cross.* With Henry Louis Gates, Jr. 2013.

PBS. *Eyes on The Prize: America's Civil Rights Years 1954-1965.* Julian Bond narrates. 2010.

PBS. *Slavery by Another Name: The Re-Enslavement of Black People in America from the Civil War to World War II.* Also available as a book from Doubleday under the same title. 2009.

PBS Indies. *Hip-Hop: Beyond Beats and Rhymes.* Byron Hurt, director. 2010.

Universal Studios. *Do the Right Thing.* Spike Lee. 1989.

Warner Bros. *Malcolm X.* Documentary narrated by James Earl Jones. 1972.

Warner Bros. *Malcolm X.* With actors Denzel Washington and Angela Bassett. 1992.

WGBH. *Africans in America: America's Journey Through Slavery.* 2000.

Organizations

American Civil Liberties Union, http://aclu.org

Association for the Study of African American Life and History, http://asalh100.org/

The James Weldon Johnson Institute for the Study of Race and Differences, Emory University, http://jamesweldonjohnson.emory.edu

National Association for the Advancement of Colored People. It has branches and student chapters in many cities. http://naacp.org

National Association for Equal Opportunity in Higher Education, http://nafeonation.org/

National Black Business Council, http://nbbc.org/

National Black Chamber of Commerce, http://nationalbcc.org/

National Urban League, http://nul.iamempowered.com/

United Negro College Fund, http://uncf.org/

Museums

Association of African American Museums, http://blackmuseums.org/

Charles H. Wright Museum of African American History, http://thewright.org/

The DuSable Museum of African American History, http://dusablemuseum.org/

The Jim Crow Museum of Racist Memorabilia, http://ferris.edu/jimcrow/

National Museum of African American History and Culture, http://nmaahc.si.edu/

National Voting Rights Museum and Institute, http://nvrmi.com/

National Civil Rights Museum, http://civilrightsmuseum.org/

Our Story

The 100 Questions and Answers series springs from the idea that good journalism should increase cross-cultural competence and understanding. Most of our guides are created by Michigan State University journalism students.

We use journalistic interviews to surface the simple, everyday questions that people have about each other but might be afraid to ask. We use research and reporting to get the answers and then put them where people can find them, read them and learn about each other.

These cultural competence guides are meant to be conversation starters. We want people to use these guides to get some baseline understanding and to feel comfortable asking more questions. We put a resources section in every guide we make and we arrange community conversations. While the guides can answer questions in private, they are meant to spark discussions.

Making these has taught us that people are not that different from each other. People share more similarities than differences. We all want the same things for ourselves and for our families. We want to be accepted, respected and understood.

Please email your thoughts and suggestions to Series Editor Joe Grimm at joe.grimm@gmail.com, at the Michigan State University School of Journalism.

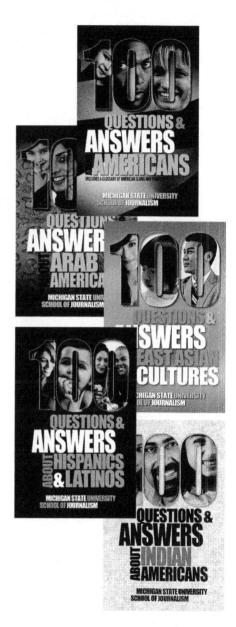

http://news.jrn.msu.edu/culturalcompetence

Related Books

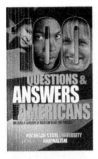

100 Questions and Answers About Americans
Michigan State University School of Journalism, 2013
This guide answers some of the first questions asked by
newcomers to the United States. Questions represent
dozens of nationalities coming from Africa, Asia,
Australia, Europe and North and South America. Good
for international students, guests and new immigrants.
http://news.jrn.msu.edu/culturalcompetence/

ISBN: 978-1-939880-20-8

100 Questions and Answers About Arab Americans
Michigan State University School of Journalism, 2014
The terror attacks of Sept. 11, 2001, propelled these Americans into a difficult position where they are victimized
twice. The guide addresses stereotypes, bias and misin-
formation. Key subjects are origins, religion, language
and customs. A map shows places of national origin.
http://news.jrn.msu.edu/culturalcompetence/

ISBN: 978-1-939880-56-7

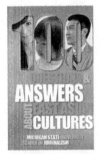

100 Questions and Answers About East Asian Cultures
Michigan State University School of Journalism, 2014
Large university enrollments from Asia prompted this
guide as an aid for understanding cultural differences. The
focus is on people from China, Japan, Korea and Taiwan
and includes Mongolia, Hong Kong and Macau. The guide
includes history, language, values, religion, foods and more.
http://news.jrn.msu.edu/culturalcompetence/

ISBN: 978-939880-50-5

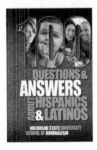

100 Questions and Answers About Hispanics & Latinos
Michigan State University School of Journalism, 2014
This group became the largest ethnic minority in the
United States in 2014 and this guide answers many of
the basic questions about it. Questions were suggested
by Hispanics and Latinos. Includes maps and charts
on origin and size of various Hispanic populations.
http://news.jrn.msu.edu/culturalcompetence/

ISBN: 978-1-939880-44-4

Print and ebooks available on Amazon.com and other retailers.

Related Books

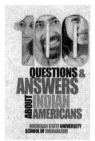

100 Questions and Answers About Indian Americans
Michigan State University School of Journalism, 2013
In answering questions about Indian Americans, this guide also addresses Pakistanis, Bangladeshis and others from South Asia. The guide covers religion, issues of history, colonization and national partitioning, offshoring and immigration, income, education, language and family.
http://news.jrn.msu.edu/culturalcompetence/

ISBN: 978-1-939880-00-0 m

100 Questions, 500 Nations: A Guide to Native America
Michigan State University School of Journalism, 2014
This guide was created in partnership with the Native American Journalists Association. The guide covers tribal sovereignty, treaties and gaming, in addition to answers about population, religion, U.S. policies and politics. The guide includes the list of federally recognized tribes.
http://news.jrn.msu.edu/culturalcompetence/

ISBN: 978-1-939880-38-3

100 Questions and Answers About Veterans
Michigan State University School of Journalism, 2015
This guide treats the more than 20 million U.S. military veterans as a cultural group with distinctive training, experiences and jargon. Graphics depict attitudes, adjustment challenges, rank, income and demographics. Includes six video interviews by Detroit Public Television.
http://news.jrn.msu.edu/culturalcompetence/

ISBN: 978-1-942011-00-2

100 Questions and Answers About American Jews
We begin by asking and answering what it means to be Jewish in America. The answers to these wide-ranging, base-level questions will ground most people and set them up for meaningful conversations with Jewish acquaintances. We cover matters of faith, food, culture, politics and stereotypes.
http://news.jrn.msu.edu/culturalcompetence/

ISBN: 978-1-942011-22-4

Print and ebooks available on Amazon.com and other retailers.

Related Books

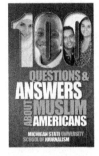

100 Questions and Answers About Muslim Americans
Michigan State University School of Journalism, 2014
This guide was done at a time of rising intolerance in the United States toward Muslims. The guide describes the presence of this religious group around the world and inside the United States. It includes audio on how to pronounce some basic Muslim words.
http://news.jrn.msu.edu/culturalcompetence/

ISBN: 978-1-939880-79-6

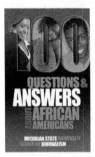

100 Questions and Answers About African Americans
Michigan State University School of Journalism, 2016
Learn about the racial issues that W.E.B. DuBois said in 1900 would be the big challenge for the 20th century. This guide explores Black and African American identity, history, language, contributions and more. Learn more about current issues in American cities and campuses.
http://news.jrn.msu.edu/culturalcompetence/

ISBN: 978-1-942011-19-4

THE NEW BULLYING

HOW SOCIAL MEDIA, SOCIAL EXCLUSION, LAWS AND SUICIDE CHANGED BULLYING

The New Bullying
Bullying has changed considerably. This book is intended to document that change. Among the changes that were examined are the rise of cyberbullying, social exclusion as a form of bullying, new laws about school bullying, computer crimes and threats and a growing willingness on the part of the public to talk about bullying and its perceived connection to suicide and violence, especially in schools.

ISBN: 978-1-934879-63-4

Print and ebooks available on Amazon.com and other retailers.

Lightning Source UK Ltd.
Milton Keynes UK
UKOW05f1605120717
305175UK00002B/576/P